How My Heart Works

by Ulrik Hvass

Illustrated by Volker Theinhardt

VIKING KESTREL

6

If a doctor wants to listen to your heart, he puts a stethoscope on your chest. Ask him to let you put the stethoscope on and then you can listen to your own heart. But why does your heart beat and what does it do?

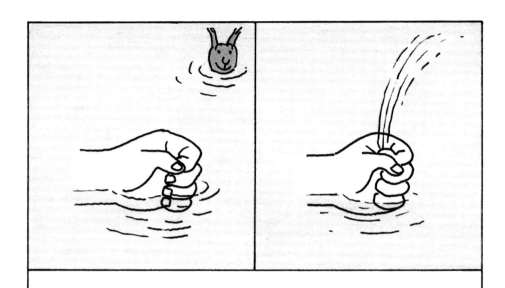

The heart pushes your blood all around your body. A simple experiment will show you how it works. Fill a sink or handbasin with water. Cup your fingers and put your hand half into the water. Then quickly close your hand: water will squirt out. Your heart works in the same sort of way.

Your heart is rather like a reservoir that keeps filling and emptying itself. Your heart works nonstop all through your life!

How big is your heart? It's about the same size as your two fists held together.

9

Now try another experiment using a sink or basin of water. When you squirt the water out of one hand, hold the other hand just above. You'll feel the force of the water. But how can you feel the spurt of blood when your heart empties itself?

Put your hand on your throat. You'll feel a beat near your thumb and one by your fingers. This beating comes from the arteries in your neck. Arteries are tubes which carry blood from the heart to all parts of your body. If an artery is near your skin, you can feel it beating. Try to find some other arteries.

11

How does the blood travel back to the heart? It's carried in a different set of tubes called veins. Look at the veins on your wrist. If you put a finger on one of them, you won't feel a beat as you did when you felt an artery. Can you find any other veins on your body?

Veins are often easier to see on elderly people. Look at the backs of their hands.

Here's a picture showing the main arteries and veins of the body. See if you can find the arteries that you've felt beating and the veins that you've noticed. Of course you won't be able to feel arteries or see veins that are deep inside you!

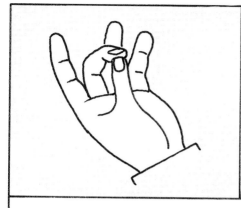
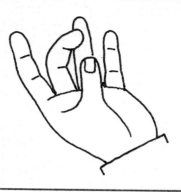

How does blood move from the arteries into the veins? These two sets of tubes are joined together by lots of tiny tubes, thinner even than one of your hairs. These tiny tubes are called capillaries. If you press the tips of your finger and thumb together, you'll see that the tips go pale. This is because the blood can't get through the capillaries. If you move your finger and thumb apart, then their color comes back quickly. Blood is moving through the capillaries again.

If you fall and hurt yourself and bleed, you'll see that that blood is bright red.

But when a doctor takes a blood test, he takes blood from a vein and that blood is dark red. What has happened to the blood to make it change color?

The bright red blood in the arteries supplies your body with fuel to make it work properly. It's like this red van that is delivering supplies to the factory. A blue van is leaving the factory with new products made in the factory.

In the same way the dark red or "blue" blood, which travels along the veins back to the heart, carries the products made by your body. This unloading of supplies from the arteries and loading of products into the veins takes place in the capillaries.

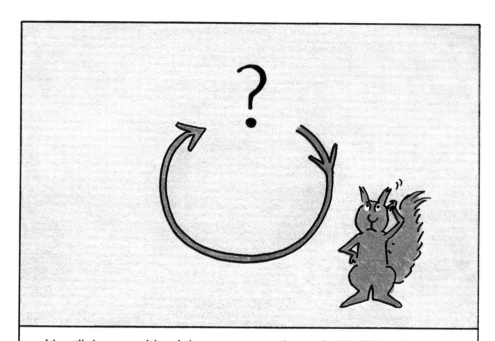

It's still the same blood that goes around your body. It's bright red when it leaves your heart but dark red or "blue" when it returns to the heart. So how does it become bright red again before going back into the arteries?

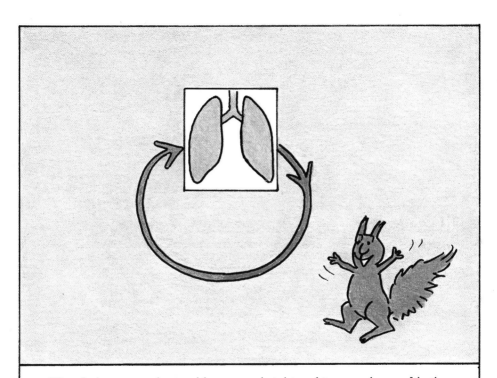

Blood changes color and becomes bright red in your lungs. It's the oxygen in the air you breathe that reddens the blood.

How is your heart made? It's formed of two pumps which are side by side. One pump sends the bright red blood around the body and the other pump sends the dark red blood toward the lungs. The two pumps are joined together and fill and empty themselves at the same time. The two pumps together are called "the heart."

The heart is a very strong pump. It can still make the blood go around your body whatever position you are in.

How often does your heart beat? Look at a watch for one minute and count the number of beats you can feel on an artery. This is what the doctor does when he takes your pulse.

24

After you've been running, do another count of the number of beats you can feel on your artery for one minute. What do you notice?

Your heart beats faster when you run. It beats slower when you sleep. Your heart works all by itself and you can't tell it what to do.

Your heart is very important to your body. Keep it healthy by exercising and by avoiding dangers to your heart such as smoking and overeating.

What do you now know about your heart? It's a pump which makes your blood travel along your arteries and veins. Your heart sends blood to all the parts of your body.

28

VIKING KESTREL

Viking Penguin Inc., 40 West 23rd Street, New York, New York 10010, U.S.A.
Penguin Books Ltd, Harmondsworth, Middlesex, England
Penguin Books Australia Ltd, Ringwood, Victoria, Australia
Penguin Books Canada Limited, 2801 John Street, Markham, Ontario, Canada L3R 1B4
Penguin Books (N.Z.) Ltd, 182-190 Wairau Road, Auckland 10, New Zealand

First published in France as *La Circulation du Sang* by
Éditions du Centurion, 1986. © 1986, Éditions du Centurion, Paris.
This English-language edition first published in 1986 by Viking Penguin Inc.
Published simultaneously in Canada
Printed in France by Offset Aubin, Poitiers
1   2   3   4   5   90   89   88   87   86

Library of Congress catalog card number: 86-40006
(CIP data available)
ISBN 0-670-81197-1